THE CROWD GOES WILD

CARTOONS & STORIES
BY
MICHAEL MASLIN

A FIRESIDE BOOK
PUBLISHED BY SIMON & SCHUSTER INC.
NEW YORK LONDON TORONTO SYDNEY TOKYO

Fireside
Simon & Schuster Building
Rockefeller Center
1230 Avenue of the Americas
New York, New York 10020

Manufactured in the United States of America

10 9 8 7 6 5 4 3 2 1

Library of Congress Cataloging in Publication Data

Maslin, Michael.
    The crowd goes wild.

    "A Fireside book."
    1. American wit and humor, Pictorial. I. Title.
NC1429.M4247A4 1989   741.5'973   88-24405
ISBN 0-671-66337-2 (pbk.)

FOR
CAROL, BERT, BRUCE,
MATTHEW, SARA AND BABAR

"Victor couldn't make it."

"*With just a little luck, we may be able to coax my husband out of his shell tonight.*"

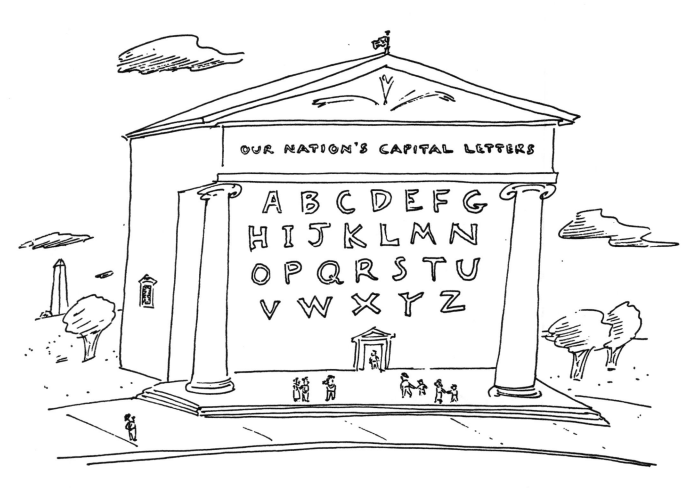

"We've traveled far, but we've never traveled wide."

SHRUB PUB

ANT ALERT

THE FIRST ANT ALERT SOUNDED LAST FRIDAY, BUT NO ONE PAID IT MUCH ATTENTION. AFTER ALL, WHAT HARM COULD AN ANT DO ANYONE?

THE FIRST ANT ALERT WAS A FALSE ONE, BUT THE NEXT DAY — A SATURDAY — IT SOUNDED AGAIN, AND THIS TIME IT WAS FOR REAL. ANTS DROPPED FROM THE TOPS OF TALL BUILDINGS, SOMETIMES INJURING INNOCENT PEOPLE ON THE SIDEWALKS BELOW.

BY SUNDAY NIGHT, EVERY ANT ALERT SHELTER IN THE CITY WAS FILLED WITH FRIGHTENED CITIZENS. THE CHIEF OF POLICE WAS QUOTED AS SAYING, " THESE ANTS AREN'T KIDDING. WHEN THEY JUMP FROM BUILDINGS, THEY'RE INTENT ON HITTING PEDESTRIANS."

"Can I put you on our mailing list?"

"Back home he's in over his head."

"I'm inconsistent—but it's a consistent inconsistency."

"Thank you, that will be all—you may hop down."

"*The doorbell is over here. You've been ringing chewing gum.*"

"Is it just me, or is everybody a comedian?"

"*I'll be back right after <u>these</u> subliminal messages.*"

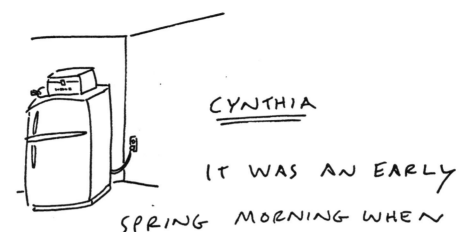

CYNTHIA

IT WAS AN EARLY SPRING MORNING WHEN CYNTHIA PULLED HER REFRIGERATOR OUT FROM THE WALL AND DISCOVERED A 1973 GIRL SCOUTS CALENDAR COVERED WITH DUST. SHE SIGHED, PUSHED THE REFRIGERATOR BACK AGAINST THE WALL, THEN WENT OUT SHOPPING.

"*Can you take an hour for lunch or are you still chained to that desk?*"

"When I say 'jump,' I expect everybody to jump."

"*I should mention that your dinners come with a polka.*"

DOO-WOP COPS

"*There are a hundred-and-one kinds of doughnuts at doughnut city. Bavarian cream is just one of them.*"

ANATOMY OF A PILLOW FIGHT

"*Are you willing to be retrained?*"

"Marge, I believe we've come to the right place."

"Stop talking nonsense, Roger—you know you're almost everything to me."

FASHION STATEMENTS

"AIMÉE IS WEARING A CREPE FUR-LINED SOMERSET COUPE. DAZZLING, AND DARING."

"GWEN'S WEARING UNSTYMIED PUMPS AND SHELLED CHIFFON BOXER REBELLION-ERA TROUSERS WITH A SIMPLE SASH."

"LIA SPORTS A CLEVERLY WRAPPED QUILTED CANAPÉ, AND AN ORANGE DE SOUPE. HER BELT IS HALF-PINCHED GEISER SUEDE."

"JACKIE'S WEARING THE WALTER FLARED VEST WITH REVERSIBLE POCKET. SHE'S HOLDING AN ARMED EVENING PURSE OF GULLIBLE LINEN."

"KEVIN'S WHALE SHIRT FEATURES AN OXFORD UPSTAIRS AFTERNOON-TO-TEA TRIANGULAR COLLAR. HIS SOCKS ARE ANKLE HIGH, AND SEWN PURELY BY COINCIDENCE."

"*This town is lousy with good guys.*"

"*Due to the relatively entertaining nature of the program you are about to see, parents are advised to bring their children back into the room.*"

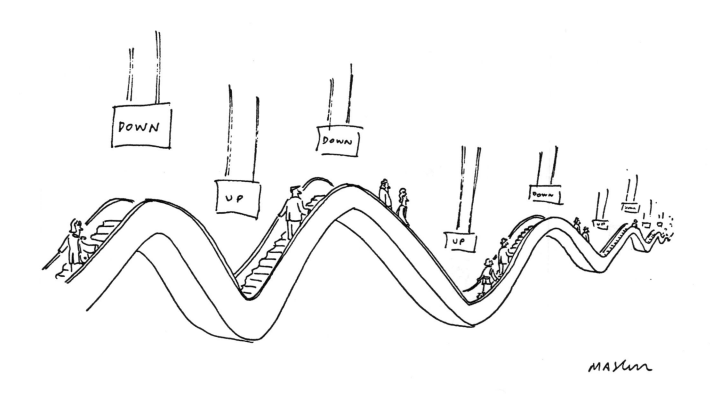

THE INFINITE ESCALATOR

"*I hear you asking me what I hear, <u>that's</u> what I hear.*"

"The following program was filmed before a live studio audience artificially sweetened with laughter."

THE CHARCOALS THAT NEVER LIT

WEEKENDS IN MAY, JUNE, JULY, AUGUST, SEPTEMBER, AND THE GOOD WEEKENDS IN OCTOBER, ARTHUR NILEY WENT THROUGH HUNDREDS OF MATCHES TRYING TO LIGHT THE CHARCOALS IN HIS BARBECUE — THE CHARCOALS THAT COULDN'T BE LIT.

WITH PAPER PLATES, PLASTIC KNIVES AND SPOONS IN HAND, FAMILY, FRIENDS, AND INVITED GUESTS STOOD BY, UNABLE, OR PERHAPS UNWILLING, TO HELP.

"*I think you have to look at the whole picture. It's not just cat and mouse—it's dog and cat and cat and mouse.*"

" '*Where* is Bertram?' *There* is Bertram."

"We're entertaining skeptics."

"You're probably wondering why I rearranged you like this."

HARRY THE HARVARD MAN

HARRY THE HARVARD MAN
HAD A GREAT TAN — A COPPER TAN.
HAD RUNNING SHOES, BUT NEVER RAN.
HARRY THE HARVARD MAN.

LAUGHING STOCK

"Would today be the day you're transferring your Cole Porter collection from records to tapes?"

"*Every time I try to talk to you, you throw up a screen.*"

THEME BOWLING

"What if I told you to get out?"

THREE WISHES ▯25¢

"*I'm very very surprised—but not speechless.*"

"Police, Mr. Rimblane—looking into the disappearance of the you everyone knew."

ENDANGERED SPECIES

"Are these to go or to drip here?"

RETURNS ONLY

CHRISTMAS MORNING, FRED BENDLER HUMMED AS HE UNWRAPPED HIS PRESENT. EVERY YEAR FOR THE PAST TWELVE, HE HAD GIVEN HIMSELF SOME-THING HE ALREADY HAD SO THAT HE WOULD HAVE TO RETURN IT.

"*I thought supplies were limited.*"

"*I wish you could see yourself, if only for a minute.*"

BACK IN 5 MINUTES

"One with mustard, and one—I believe—without."

"*I would like to say something, Your Honor, and, if the court pleases, I'd like to say it with flowers.*"

TOUCAN DUET

DEAR DIARY

TODAY WE WERE STRANDED ON THE THRUWAY FOR SIX AND A HALF HOURS, JUST THREE MILES FROM HOME. IT WAS ONLY WHEN GORDON FAILED TO JOIN ME IN SINGING "WHITE CHRISTMAS" THAT I REALIZED HE HAD ALREADY MADE UP HIS MIND THAT I WAS TO BLAME FOR THE SNOW.

"We're coming up."

"*I laugh on the outside and he laughs on the inside.*"

"You're hiding something from me, Ed. What is it?"

"*The consensus is then that we're still not out of the woods.*"

"And how would you like your taste buds assaulted—by surf or by turf?"

BEAR NECESSITIES

"*I'm reminded that it's not where you're going, it's where you've been.*"

"*Everything he does is unprecedented.*"

"Since when are you invisible?"

"*This fellow began developing earmuffs as a hedge against the coming chill.*"

"What our desserts lack in quality they more than make up for in quantity."

"He's the friend of a friend of a complete stranger."

"How long has it been now, Norman, since you, personally, accepted advertising?"

POSTURE ON PARADE

"Dave—your toast!"

"Go to your rooms."

"*We're not laughing at you, Manfred—we're laughing without you.*"

TWO YEAR UPDATES

JEFF MALIWYCK, NOW LIVING IN PHILADELPHIA, STILL HAS A NERVOUS TWITCH ONLY WHEN HE'S ABOUT TO SIP HOT COFFEE.

CAROL HABOUT, THE WOMAN WHO RETRACES HER EVERY STEP, IS NOW SOMEWHERE ON THE SIDEWALKS OF MILLBURN, NEW JERSEY, HEADING BACK TO THE CORNER STORE WHERE SHE PURCHASED A PACK OF GRAPE CHEWING GUM IN 1966.

KEN DWELLERT, WHOSE LEFT EYEBROW ONCE SWELLED TO THE SIZE OF A GRAPEFRUIT, IS NOW HAPPILY REMARRIED TO THE FORMER GAIL PRESTON.

"*How long have you been interesting?*"

CONDUCTOR INSTRUCTOR

"*This is not a shakedown, Mr. Bedeker; you owe the library this money.*"

"George, I don't think we're in Massapequa any more."

TENNIS COURT

"Here's a glimpse of the me so few ever see."

"*Murston has plenty of style, but very little substance.*"

UNIMPEACHABLE SOURCE

"Something in a deep-fry for the gentleman, perhaps?"

"*Put all your money in the register, then back out of the store—slowly.*"

THE WAITING GAME

"*I'm a king, you're a king. Comparisons are inevitable.*"

NEAT AND TIDY

MR. BROWNE HAD ONLY HALF-
STOOD TO ADJUST HIS TROUSER LEGS
WHEN RUTH REACHED BEHIND HIM
TO FLUFF UP A SMALL PILLOW AND
BUFF UP THE PRESSED VELVET OF THE
SOFA.

"MY, YOU'RE NEAT AND TIDY," HE
SAID TO RUTH.

THE BLUSHING YET PRACTICAL RUTH
REPLIED, "OH, GO ON," AS SHE OFFERED
HIM A TOFFEE IN THE SHAPE OF A
TWO-CAR GARAGE.

"This is John Downey, live at the sea-quarium."

"*These daisies are still just as plastic as the day I bought them.*"

AUTOGRAPH HOUNDS

AFTER TWO WEEKS OF DRIFTING
I'VE NEARLY COMPLETED AN OUTLINE
FOR A MINI SERIES OR THREE-HOUR
SPECTACULAR BASED ON MY EXPERIENCE.

"And from this corner, blueberry pies!"

"And here, in wax, is my husband."

"*Your life can no more be carefree than it can be sugar free.*"

ALL SMILES

THURSDAY EVENING, MARTY WAS
ALL SMILES, UNTIL HE BEGAN TO CRY.
HIS TEARS WERE PLAINLY VISIBLE
AS THEY ROLLED DOWN HIS CHEEKS.
GLORIA LOOKED ON WITH LITTLE
SYMPATHY, FOR IT WAS ONLY YESTER-
DAY THAT SHE TOO HAD SLICED AN
ONION.

"*Seconds ticking away turning into minutes, minutes turning into hours, hours into days, days into weeks, weeks into months, months into years, years into decades, lifetimes—and you without a watch?*"

SHEEP MEET

GOOD FOOD
AT
MEDIEVAL
PRICES
→

JACK

JACK NILDRY FELT A
HEARTFELT LAUGH COMING
UPON HIMSELF, SO HE PREPARED
ACCORDINGLY BY PUTTING
ON A FRESHLY STARCHED
WHITE SHIRT AND A GOOD
PAIR OF PANTS.

"This year, Alf is keeping right on top of the weeds."

"We're a company called Bestrex, solving tomorrow's problems tonight, so we can take tomorrow off."

"This building is now under __very__ tight security."

"*Do you think there are gift shops, as we know them, on other planets?*"

"*Bill was once mayor.*"

"*Remember, Mr. McBreen, it's not just a job—it's something to do when you're not pursuing leisure-time activities.*"

SHOUTING MATCH

"*Am I blocking your way? Yes, no—don't know.*"

A TOUGH DECISION FOR DAN AMONG THE JARS OF JAM

"Murray has a mind tease for us."

"*John Doe, Jane Doe, and John Q. Public.*"

THE ERASABLE MR. DAN

FROM THE DAY HE WAS ABLE TO SIT UP PROPERLY IN A HIGH-BACKED CHAIR, IT WAS APPARENT THAT DANNY DILE. WAS ERASABLE.

HE GREW UP BEING CAREFUL OF THINGS. CHILDHOOD AND ADOLESCENCE WERE MARRED BY THE OCCASIONAL ERASURE OF A SNOW CAP OR MITTEN. AS AN ADULT, DANNY UNFORTUNATELY RUBBED EVERYONE HE MET THE WRONG WAY.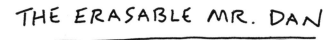

"*Ernest knows I'm going to turn on the sprinkler, but he doesn't know when—is that stress?*"

"*You know, he hasn't changed one bit since we were kids.*"

"When the music stops, there'll be one less guest."

"It's how Bix wants to be remembered—diving for pearls."

CONVERSATION PIECES

"MARK IS AN EX-SIAMESE TWIN," ALICIA WAS SAYING TO HER MOTHER, "YOU'LL REALLY LIKE HIM."

"MY SHOES!" CRIED ELSIE SCHWIPPS.

"WILL EVERYONE PLEASE, <u>PLEASE</u> BE QUIET," SHOUTED LEONARD HALLET, TREASURER.

"I CAN SEE PERFECTLY FINE," SAID MR. TWIM AS HE SWERVED HIS CAR SHARPLY TO THE RIGHT TO AVOID AN ONCOMING TRUCK.

"*Before I pass judgment, is there anything else you'd like to play?*"

"*That won't work—it's a toy.*"

A TOAST TO RETIREMENT, AND PRESENTATION
OF THE GOLD WATCH TO THE SELF-EMPLOYED MAN

"*Suddenly, in his fifty-third year, every day's a new adventure.*"

"*I don't remember first or last names—only middle names. <u>Your</u> middle name is*
Strudel."

"*May I ask what your appointment with Mr. Marsh is in reference to?*"

"Beware of the occupant."

"Garçon, Garçon."

A PUPPET A POET A PIRATE A PAUPER A PAWN AND A KING

"*Sorry, Phisley, but if I have to step on toes, I step on toes.*"

ONE MORNING

ONE MORNING, AS ANGELO LAID OUT THE CLOTHES HE'D WEAR THAT DAY, HE THOUGHT OF ANGELA— ONLY OF ANGELA. A SMILE CREASED HIS FACE WHEN IT SUDDEN- LY OCCURRED TO HIM THAT HIS CLOTHES WOULD NEVER NEED IRONING. THIS WAS LOVE. THIS WAS WASH AND WEAR.

"Marie, are we really right for each other—for this furniture?"

"At this time, Your Honor, the state would like to call forth its parade of witnesses."

"*It isn't summer until you throw me into the pool.*"

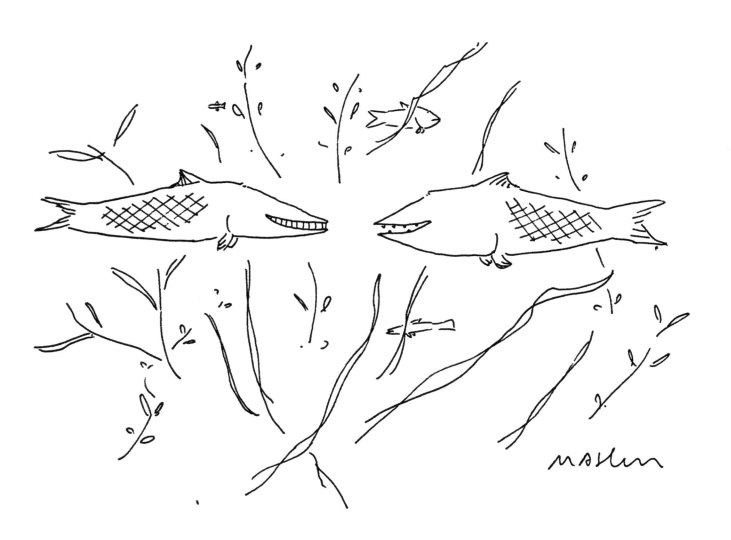

"*I suppose the first thing I was attracted to was your smile.*"

ABOUT THE AUTHOR

Michael Maslin is a cartoonist for *The New Yorker* magazine. He lives in New York with his wife, Liza Donnelly, an artist and writer. He has published two other cartoon collections, *The More the Merrier* and *The Gang's All Here!*